THE CREATIVE CURRICULUM®
FOR INFANTS, TODDLERS & TWOS

Developmental Continuum
Assessment System

Teacher's Guide

Teaching Strategies, Inc.
Washington, DC

Cover, book design, and layout: Carla Uriona
Illustrations: Jennifer Barrett O'Connell

Teaching Strategies, Inc.
P.O. Box 42243
Washington, DC 20015
www.TeachingStrategies.com
ISBN: 978-1-933021-34-8

Teaching Strategies and *The Creative Curriculum* names and logos are
registered trademarks of Teaching Strategies, Inc., Washington, DC.

The publisher and the authors cannot be held responsible for injury,
mishap, or damages incurred during the use of or because of the
information in this book. The authors recommend appropriate and
reasonable supervision at all times based on the age and capability
of each child.

Printed and bound in the United States of America
2011   2010   2009   2008   2007
10 9 8 7 6 5 4 3 2

Contents

Introduction

Interactions with other people help children learn about themselves, about relating to others, and about the world. Building trusting, responsive relationships with children is therefore the most important part of your work. To be responsive, you have to know each child well. Observation is the key to knowing a child. *The Creative Curriculum® Developmental Continuum for Infants, Toddlers & Twos* is designed to make purposeful observation part of your everyday practice, and it is the core of the Assessment System.

Using the *Developmental Continuum* will help you observe children in the context of everyday routines and experiences. You will be able to assess each child's current level of development and to think about likely next steps. Then you can plan for each child and the group. As you learn about each child's strengths, interests, and developmental timetable, you can use the information and strategies in *The Creative Curriculum* to decide how to build responsive relationships and to offer experiences that promote each child's development and learning.

The *Developmental Continuum* and related materials are available as either a Toolkit with paper forms or as a fully integrated, Web-enabled system, CreativeCurriculum.net. Throughout this *Teacher's Guide* you will notice a symbol. The text that follows it describes how CreativeCurriculum.net can help you with assessment, reporting, and planning tasks.

How to Use This *Teacher's Guide*

This *Teacher's Guide* explains the value of thinking about child development as a continuous, step-by-step process. It introduces the goals and objectives of *The Creative Curriculum for Infants, Toddlers & Twos* and *The Creative Curriculum Developmental Continuum for Infants, Toddlers & Twos*. The *Teacher's Guide* outlines the process of ongoing assessment, including collecting and analyzing facts, and evaluating children's progress. It also explains how to plan for each child and the group based on what you learn.

In addition to this *Teacher's Guide*, you will be using the following materials:

- *The Creative Curriculum Developmental Continuum for Infants, Toddlers & Twos* shows developmental steps (with examples) for each of 21 objectives and shows how the objectives are related to four goals in four developmental areas.

- *The Creative Curriculum for Infants, Toddlers & Twos: Goals and Objectives at a Glance* also shows the developmental areas, goals, and objectives but omits the steps and examples in order to serve as a quick reference. This poster can be displayed in your classroom for easy reference.

- The *Individual Child Profile* is used to document each child's progress at three or four times, known as checkpoints, during the year.

- The *Observation Tracking Form* is a record-keeping form to help you remember which children you have observed and when.

- The *Child Planning Form* is used to record current information and your plans for each child.

- The *Group Planning Form* is used to record a weekly group plan that is based on information from all of your *Child Planning Forms*.

- The *Family Conference Form* is used to summarize a child's progress, record information and ideas from the family, and plan together to support the child's next steps.

The *Teacher's Guide* helps you implement an ongoing assessment process as you use *The Creative Curriculum for Infants, Toddlers & Twos*. It has the following sections:

The Creative Curriculum for Infants, Toddlers & Twos: **Goals and Objectives.** This section introduces the goals and objectives of the curriculum and of the *Developmental Continuum for Infants, Toddlers & Twos*. For each of 21 objectives, the *Developmental Continuum* shows progressive developmental steps for children ages 2–36 months.

Preparing for Assessment. This section explains how to get ready by setting up systems for collecting and organizing observation notes and portfolio items.

Collecting Facts. This section describes the first phase in linking program planning and assessment: learning as much as possible about each child. You collect facts by observing children throughout the day and documenting what you see and hear.

Analyzing Facts and Evaluating Children's Progress. Observation notes and portfolio items contain a wealth of information that must be analyzed and evaluated so you can determine each child's level of development related to particular objectives. For this part of the assessment process, you use the *Developmental Continuum*, the *Goals and Objectives at a Glance*, the *Observation Tracking Form*, and the *Individual Child Profile*.

Planning for Each Child and the Group. The information you have about each child in relation to the objectives of *The Creative Curriculum* enables you to develop a plan to meet the child's needs. You review observation information to complete the *Child Planning Form* and the *Group Planning Form* on a weekly basis. You review and summarize what you have learned about a child on the *Family Conference Form*, and then you meet with families to exchange information and plan next steps.

The chart on the opposite page illustrates the ongoing relationship between assessment and curriculum.

Promoting High-Quality Assessment. This section shows how to establish interrater reliability within programs using the *Developmental Continuum* Assessment System. It also discusses use of the Assessment System in early intervention programs.

Linking Curriculum and Assessment—The Ongoing Cycle

Planning for Assessment

- Become familiar with *The Creative Curriculum® Developmental Continuum for Infants, Toddlers & Twos*
- Set up a systematic way to observe, document, and organize your notes
- Set up a portfolio for each child

1 Collecting Facts

Observe and document children's learning

- Observe children with curriculum objectives in mind
- Document what you see and hear
- Collect portfolio samples over time

2 Analyzing & Evaluating Facts

Analyze facts

- Sort observation notes by goal for each child
- Label each note and portfolio sample with the number of each objective that applies to the observation

Evaluate children's progress

- Review observation notes and portfolio items
- Use the *Developmental Continuum* to select the step that best describes each child's level of development for each of the 21 objectives
- Enter information on the *Individual Child Profile* at each checkpoint

3 Planning for Each Child & the Group

Ongoing planning

- Review and summarize ongoing observations, keeping the *Developmental Continuum* in mind
- Enter information on the *Child Planning* and *Group Planning* forms
- Implement your plans and continue to observe the child

4 Sharing Children's Progress

With families

- Summarize each child's progress on the *Family Conference Form* at each checkpoint
- Meet with families to share information and jointly plan next steps

With others

- Collect and summarize data if needed to prepare reports (e.g., program administrators, funders)

©2006 Teaching Strategies, Inc., PO Box 42243, Washington, DC 20015; www.TeachingStrategies.com

I. *The Creative Curriculum for Infants, Toddlers & Twos:* Goals and Objectives

To provide quality care, you need to know how children develop and what you want them to learn. The goals and objectives of *The Creative Curriculum* are organized in four developmental areas: social/emotional, physical, cognitive, and language. They address the important aspects of a child's development and learning that can be influenced by the care and education you provide. The goals and objectives will help you

- understand how infants, toddlers, and twos typically develop and what they can learn in a high-quality program

- focus your ongoing observations and build trusting, caring relationships as you come to appreciate what each child knows and can do

- become aware of each child's strengths as well as areas that need extra support

- use the information and strategies in *The Creative Curriculum* to make decisions about the environment, about routines and experiences, and about what to say and do in order to help individual children develop and learn

The Creative Curriculum for Infants, Toddlers & Twos and *The Creative Curriculum Developmental Continuum for Infants, Toddlers & Twos* share the same goals and objectives for children's development and learning. Each of the four goals corresponds to an area of child development:

- Goal 1: To learn about self and others—Social/Emotional development

- Goal 2: To learn about moving—Physical development

- Goal 3: To learn about the world—Cognitive development

- Goal 4: To learn about communicating—Language development

The *Developmental Continuum* shows the objectives that are related to each developmental area or goal, and it outlines the developmental steps (with examples) that are related to each objective. The *Goals and Objectives At A Glance* can be found on page 29.

Goal 1: To Learn About Self and Others

Young children are learning who they are and how to relate to others. By forming attachments with others, children learn to feel valued and important. Through the trust they develop with their families and teachers, they become confident and secure. Trust and security enable them to venture into the world and to balance independence with interdependence. Babies and toddlers begin to develop personal care skills as they take increasing control of their lives, e.g., as they pull their knees to their chests when placed on the diapering table and as they accept or reject spoonfuls of food.

Learning about themselves also includes learning about feelings and how to manage them. As children learn to calm themselves and to express their feelings appropriately, they gain confidence in themselves as individuals. They also learn to regulate their behavior, first responding to adult cues and eventually knowing what behavior is expected. Of course, as toddlers and twos, they sometimes test limits. Their growing ability to empathize with others' feelings develops along with other social skills. As children learn to play with other children, to cooperate with others, and to empathize, they become members of a social community.

"To learn about self and others" includes these seven objectives:

- Objective 1: Trusts known, caring adults
- Objective 2: Regulates own behavior
- Objective 3: Manages own feelings
- Objective 4: Responds to others' feelings with growing empathy
- Objective 5: Plays with other children
- Objective 6: Learns to be a member of a group
- Objective 7: Uses personal care skills

Goal 2: To Learn About Moving

Young children's physical development is intertwined with cognitive and social/emotional development. As children explore their environment and develop thinking and social skills, they also develop gross motor and fine motor skills. The reverse is also true.

Infants, toddlers, and twos develop basic gross motor skills like sitting, crawling, walking, and running. They also gain balance and learn to coordinate their hand and foot movements. With practice, they begin to catch, throw, pedal, and steer.

Young children refine their fine motor skills as they do such things as poke playdough, hold a paintbrush, drink from a sippy cup, and pull off a hat. Coordination and skill evolve with practice.

"To learn about moving" includes these two objectives:

- Objective 8: Demonstrates basic gross motor skills
- Objective 9: Demonstrates basic fine motor skills

Goal 3: To Learn About the World

Babies are curious about everything. They explore and experiment to learn how things work. They explore the properties of objects by looking at, feeling, mouthing, banging, and shaking them. They begin to understand that things can be grouped, and they sort beads, Duplos®, pegs, and other toys into piles by color. They learn how objects can be used, for example, that bottles and cups are used for drinking.

Infants, toddlers, and twos develop a beginning understanding of cause and effect, discovering that their actions can make things happen. Their ability to focus and stay engaged in a task grows. They become adept at solving simple problems, as their trial and error attempts become purposeful plans. Through imitation and pretend play, children learn about symbolic thinking as well as about social roles and the use of objects. This prepares them for learning to read and write and for future academic success.

"To learn about the world" includes these six objectives:

- Objective 10: Sustains attention
- Objective 11: Understands how objects can be used
- Objective 12: Shows a beginning understanding of cause and effect
- Objective 13: Shows a beginning understanding that things can be grouped
- Objective 14: Uses problem-solving strategies
- Objective 15: Engages in pretend play

Goal 4: To Learn About Communicating

The development of speech and language is one of the major achievements of the first few years of life. To be able to comprehend and produce standard speech and to begin to understand the uses of language are astonishing accomplishments. Babies listen to the sounds of their home language or languages and respond by cooing, babbling, and ultimately saying their first words. They develop new vocabulary, put words together as sentences, and learn the uses of language as they participate in conversations and as others read to them.

Through oral language and interaction with books and environmental print, children gain a foundation for learning to read and write. When they explore books on their own and listen as books are read aloud, they gain an awareness of print, play with the sounds of language, and are encouraged to find meaning in books and print. Giving children opportunities to scribble on paper also helps them learn about written language. These early years set a pattern for enjoying and succeeding with reading and writing.

"To learn about communicating" includes these six objectives:

- Objective 16: Develops receptive language
- Objective 17: Develops expressive language
- Objective 18: Participates in conversations
- Objective 19: Enjoys books and being read to
- Objective 20: Shows an awareness of pictures and print
- Objective 21: Experiments with drawing and writing

How to Read the *Developmental Continuum*

Children do not master a skill or objective all at once. Instead, development typically follows sequential steps. For this reason, the *Developmental Continuum* shows five developmental steps for each of 21 objectives and gives three increasingly mature examples to illustrate each step.

The figure below shows one objective, Objective 18, "Participates in conversations," as an example. It is one of the six objectives related to Goal 4, "To learn about communicating." The examples for each step give you an idea of what you may observe in your classroom.

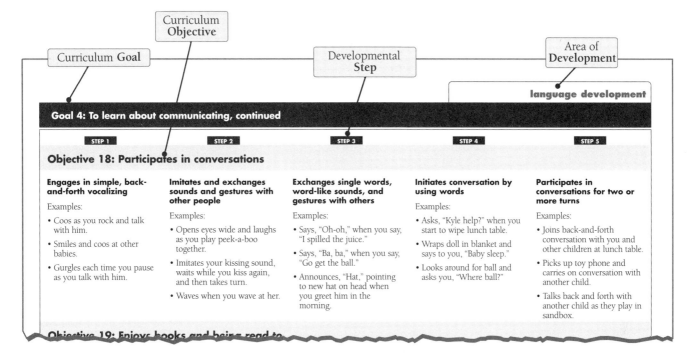

For each objective, you will need to decide whether a child is at Step 1, 2, 3, 4, or 5. Step 1 is a beginning stage of typical development, and Step 5 is the most advanced stage for children under age 3.

Children demonstrate their mastery of skills in a variety of ways. Because the examples presented in the *Developmental Continuum* are sample behaviors, you may or may not see these particular behaviors when you observe the children in your care. Look for behaviors that are of a similar type and skill level.

As you become familiar with the *Developmental Continuum*, you will see that the examples for several objectives are very similar. For instance, several examples involve a child's playing with a doll or smiling and babbling at you. This is because a particular behavior and your observation note relate to more than one objective. Similarly, a step sometimes relates to more than one objective. For instance, the step, "Explores objects, using all senses" relates to Objective 11, "Understands how objects can be used," and to Objective 13, "Shows a beginning understanding that things can be grouped."

Appreciating Individual Differences

The *Developmental Continuum* helps you understand how children typically develop and learn. Many things influence a child's development. Understanding individual differences, such as a child's home culture, life circumstances, and temperament, can also help you find other appropriate indicators of a child's developmental level. For example, Abby's mother explains to Brooks that she prefers to feed Abby (14 months), rather than have Abby feed herself. She believes that, in this way, she shows Abby how much she loves her and that it is important for people to depend on and help each other. Brooks knows that this culturally-supported practice may affect what Brooks can observe about Abby's personal care skills (Objective 7) and fine motor skills (Objective 9). Brooks decides she will look for other ways to observe Abby's growing abilities in these areas, such as putting a shirt in her cubby or picking up large beads.

In another example, Mercedes knows that children's temperaments affect the way they relate to new situations and people. Matthew (22 months) is naturally slow to adapt. Because of this, Mercedes is not concerned that he has just recently reached Step 3 on Objective 1, "Trusts known caring adults," although he is at Step 4 on many other objectives. Mercedes knows that, with continued support and close, nurturing relationships, Matthew will eventually feel more comfortable around new people.

The Value of Looking at Objectives on a Continuum

Looking at goals and objectives on a continuum has these advantages:

- Major changes take place during the first three years of life. A continuum enables you to see progress along the way.

- A continuum helps you determine each child's level of development at a particular time and what steps are expected next as the child progresses toward achieving each objective.

- The information enables you to plan experiences that build on children's strengths and interests.

- The sequence of steps fosters a positive approach to caring and teaching by outlining what children can do and suggesting what comes next, rather than by emphasizing what they cannot do yet.

- The information can be shared with families in a way that reassures them about their child's progress.

II. Preparing for Assessment

This *Teacher's Guide* is designed to help you understand how to observe, assess, and plan for the children in your care during everyday routines and experiences. Before you begin using the Assessment System, read the entire *Teacher's Guide*. Make sure you understand the *Developmental Continuum*, how to write observation notes that are objective rather than judgmental, how to evaluate information so you can decide which step accurately reflects a child's level of development, and how to use the various forms in the assessment process. Next, set up a system for taking and organizing observation notes and work samples.

Documenting what children do and say takes time. If you have a system for recording your observations and storing observation notes, documentation will be easier.

Setting Up a System for Taking Notes

Keep your system as simple as possible so it helps you. Here are some ideas that have worked for other teachers.

> **Use mailing labels or sticky notes** to record your observations. At the beginning of the day, place three or four notes or labels with the names of the children whom you wish to observe on a clipboard and keep it handy. At the end of the day, transfer the completed notes or labels to each child's file.

> **Draw a grid on the inside of a folder.** Include 3–6 boxes or as many as the number of children in your primary care group. Write a different child's name in each box on the grid. Keep sticky notes in your pocket or near the folder. After writing an observation note about a child, place it in the box with that child's name. Make duplicate folders for various areas of the room.

> **Develop your own system of shorthand** so you can record information quickly. Write brief notes, using short phrases and abbreviating whenever possible. You can emphasize words by underlining them.

You do not need to write an observation note for every child, every day. You may find it easiest to focus on one or two children per day. Remember that you do not need to record everything that happens and everything a child says and does.

Organizing Observation Notes

You also need a system for organizing your observation notes. While there are a variety of ways to organize them, many teachers find the following approach useful:

1. Purchase a large loose-leaf notebook and include a tabbed divider for each child in your group. In the front of the binder, place a copy of the *Goals and Objectives at a Glance* inside a protective plastic cover. Next, insert a copy of the *Developmental Continuum* to use as a reference.

2. Behind each tab in the notebook, insert an *Individual Child Profile* and four blank pages. At the top of each blank page, write one of these headings: *To learn about self and others*, *To learn about moving*, *To learn about the world*, or *To learn about communicating*. You might want to use a different color of paper for each goal. Later, you will use these pages to sort and store your observation notes for each child.

The *Observation Tracking Form* will help you record which children you have observed and the related objectives. It includes spaces for the children in your primary care group. Updating it on a regular basis will enable you to focus your observations and to follow children's progress.

 If you are using CreativeCurriculum.net, first set up your classes. Once organized, they are your online filing cabinet and include a file for each child. All of your observation notes, portfolio items, family journal entries, and forms are stored in this electronic file folder. You can retrieve all of this information throughout the assessment and planning process.

Creating a Portfolio for Each Child

A portfolio is a collection of items that document a child's interests, skills, accomplishments, and approaches to learning. These create a profile of a child and his learning over time. Portfolios for infants, toddlers, and twos contain items such as photographs, scribbles, paintings, and video or audio clips.

At the beginning of the year, think of two or three types of items that would be good for documenting growth in each goal area. Plan to collect similar samples periodically throughout the year. For example, you might include photographs that capture a child's involvement in social activities, videotapes of a child using physical skills, videotapes of a child engaged in pretend play or reading a book, and audiotapes of a child's language. Next, consider storage. Pocket folders are fine for photographs, drawings, and scribbles, but you might want to use accordion files or shallow boxes for items such as paintings or video- and audiotapes. You can even create a larger file folder by folding and stapling tagboard.

III. Collecting Facts

Once you have established a system for taking and organizing observation notes and for collecting and storing portfolio items, you can begin documenting what you see. We call this *collecting facts*. You collect facts by observing children and documenting what they do and say, by maintaining a portfolio for each child, and by exchanging information with families.

Observing What Children Do and Say

Observation is one of your most important teaching tools because it helps you learn about each child. *The Creative Curriculum* goals and objectives will help you focus your observations. The more familiar you are with the 21 objectives, the more purposefully you can observe children. Post a copy of the goals and objectives where you can see it easily or keep a copy on a handy clipboard.

Most of your observations of children occur during daily routines and experiences, and they yield a wealth of information about a child or a group of children. Work with your co-teachers to decide whether you will observe the children for whom you are the primary caregiver or whether you will observe all of the children in the group. You may wish to follow one child for a period of time and record all of the behaviors that relate to a particular goal or area of development. Another approach is to observe a small group of children, write your observation notes, and later identify the related objectives. Both approaches yield rich information to help you plan learning opportunities. You will also find that, as you become increasingly familiar with the *Developmental Continuum*, note taking will become easier.

To determine how each child in your program is progressing, you must conduct observations that relate to all 21 objectives. This does not mean that you need to conduct separate observations of each child for each objective. One observation yields information about many objectives.

Think about how much you might learn from one simple observation. Imagine that you are observing a two year old who takes a picture book off a shelf and looks at the pictures on each page while sitting next to another child who is also looking at a book. This observation gives you information about these objectives:

- Objective 5: Plays with other children
- Objective 9: Demonstrates basic fine motor skills
- Objective 19: Enjoys books and being read to
- Objective 20: Shows an awareness of pictures and print

Documenting Your Observations Accurately and Objectively

To be useful, observation notes must be objective and factual. When your notes include words like *fussy, upset, hyperactive,* or *aggressive,* they reveal your interpretation of what a child did or said, not simply the facts. Judgmental words may or may not accurately record what took place. You need to collect a series of objective, factual observations in order to understand the child's behavior. Taking objective notes requires practice. Below are two examples of objective observational notes.

Valisha— 9/8

V picked up scissors; began to cut paper. Moved scissor blades back and forth. Couldn't get paper to cut; scissors crumpled paper. V frowned and dropped scissors on table. V stared at scissors; said nothing. Picked up same piece of paper. Began tearing it with hands.

Willard—10/30

Crawled to bookshelf. Put both hands on shelf; pulled himself to standing. Pulled two books off shelf. Turned around and looked at me. I shook my head, "No." Then W lowered himself to floor and crawled to nearby truck.

Maintaining a Portfolio for Each Child

During the year, you will continue to add items to each child's portfolio. Be sure to date each item and write a short note about what was occurring when the sample was created. For example, a photo of Abby (14 months) washing dolls does not tell you that Abby carefully wiped the doll's eyes with a cloth, saying, "No." It also does not show that, when she finished washing the doll, she got a towel and patted it dry. You need to supplement the photo or portfolio item with a note that completes the record of what the child did and said.

Remember that each portfolio item can reveal a great deal of information about the child. For example, a photo of Abby washing baby dolls in a basin reveals this information:

- She uses one hand to hold the doll and the other hand to manipulate the soap, cloth, water, and towel (Objective 9, "Demonstrates basic fine motor skills").

- She can focus on an activity of choice (Objective 10, "Sustains attention").

- She knows how to use familiar objects such as soap, water, and a basin (Objective 11, "Understands how objects can be used").

- She uses objects in pretend play as they are used in real life (Objective 15, "Engages in pretend play").

- She uses single words to communicate (Objective 17, "Develops expressive language").

 If you are using CreativeCurriculum.net, you can type your observation notes into the system. You can also scan photos and samples of children's scribbles and art, and you can add video and audio clips (up to 2 MB per file). You can then retrieve your observation notes and portfolio samples to help evaluate which step best reflects the child's level of development.

IV. Analyzing Facts and Evaluating Children's Progress

The next part of the assessment process involves reorganizing your notes and portfolio items and determining what they tell you about a child's progress toward achieving each of the 21 objectives. These tools will help you do this:

- *The Creative Curriculum for Infants, Toddlers & Twos: Goals and Objectives at a Glance*
- *The Creative Curriculum Developmental Continuum for Infants, Toddlers & Twos*
- *Individual Child Profile*
- *Observation Tracking Form*

Analyzing Facts

To analyze your observation notes, you will need to organize your notes about each child. Sort them according to the goal area to which they most closely relate. At the end of each day, or at least several times a week, take out the group loose-leaf notebook you created and follow these steps:

1. Collect all the notes you have about one child.

2. Review the notes for one child at a time and decide to what goal the observation note most closely relates. You may want to make a copy of the note if it applies to more than one goal.

3. Affix the notes to the appropriate pages in each child's section of your notebook.

As you review each note, ask yourself, "What does this tell me about the child's development and learning?" Refer to the objectives and decide which apply. Record the numbers of the objectives on the note or on the back of the portfolio item.

Valisha— 9/8

V picked up scissors; began to cut paper. Moved scissor blades back and forth. Couldn't get paper to cut; scissors crumpled paper. V frowned and dropped scissors on table. V stared at scissors; said nothing. Picked up same piece of paper. Began tearing it with hands.

#9, #3, #10, #11, #14

Here is how you might analyze the sample observation notes that were presented earlier.

The observation note about Valisha is clearly related to Objective 9, "Demonstrates basic fine motor skills." You would write #9 on the note and place it in Valisha's section of the notebook, on the page headed "To learn about moving." The note also gives information about Valisha's emotional development, particularly about Objective 3, "Manages own feelings." You would also record #3 on a copy, and file it on Valisha's page headed "To learn about self and others."

Then you would write #10, #11, and #14 on another copy and file it on Valisha's page headed "To learn about the world." This is because the behavior you documented is also related to those objectives ("Sustains attention," "Understands how objects can be used," and "Uses problem-solving strategies").

> ## Willard—10/30
>
> Crawled to bookshelf. Put both hands on shelf; pulled himself to standing. Pulled two books off shelf. Turned around and looked at me. I shook my head, "No." Then W lowered himself to floor and crawled to nearby truck.
>
> #8, #2, #16

The observation note about Willard also provides information about at least three objectives. It gives you information about Objective 8, "Demonstrates basic gross motor skills"; Objective 2, "Regulates own behavior"; and Objective 16, "Develops receptive language." Again, you might place the note in the observation notebook under physical development, but it can also be used to evaluate Willard on Objectives 2 and 16.

 Once you have typed your observation note in CreativeCurriculum.net, you can also select the numbers of the related objectives.

Evaluating Each Child's Progress

Evaluating a child's progress means thinking about all 21 objectives and deciding which developmental step reflects a child's level of development for each. You need to consider all the documentation you have collected, including your observation notes and the child's portfolio. Examine the information for each objective. Using the *Developmental Continuum*, think about what the child did and said, and decide which of the five steps best represents the child's skill level for the objective. If you are in a group setting with co-teachers, you may want to do this together or at least discuss your findings.

To understand the evaluation process, consider the observation note about Willard that was presented previously. This note gives you information about Objective 2, "Regulates own behavior." The note reminds you that Willard looked at you after taking books from the shelf. He did not pull more books off the shelf after you shook your head, "No." In terms of Objective 2, this note records an example of a Step 2 behavior, "Uses others' facial expressions, gestures, or voices to guide own behavior."

You would not make a final determination about Willard's developmental step on the basis of this single observation. You would review several observation notes and any portfolio items related to Objective 2. If the additional notes and items show Step 2 behaviors, you would choose Step 2 of Objective 2.

As you review your observation notes and portfolio items that relate to a particular objective, you may find that the child's behavior corresponded to more than one step.

These guidelines will help you to select the appropriate step of the objective:

- Select the step that describes the child's behavior or skill level most consistently.

- If a child is just beginning to exhibit skills for a step, place the child at the previous step.

- Look at the dates on the observation notes and portfolio items. If notes taken early in the checkpoint period indicate a lower step than notes taken later in the checkpoint period, and if the child consistently exhibits skills at a higher step now, choose the higher step.

Evaluate each child's development on all 21 objectives in this way. While a child's skill level is likely to be the same for many objectives, children may be more advanced in one developmental area than another. For example, a particular child may be at Step 1 for one objective and Step 2 for another. If a child does not seem to be making progress or even regresses in a particular developmental area on a number of objectives, consider whether the child needs to be observed further and screened for possible developmental delays. In this instance, a tool designed for screening, rather than the *Developmental Continuum*, which is designed for ongoing assessment, can help you set in motion a process for identifying a possible developmental delay or disability.

At your program's checkpoints, use the *Individual Child Profile* to record your decisions about the steps that describe the child's development. Although you observe children every day, we suggest that you formally complete the *Individual Child Profile* for each child three or four times a year, coinciding with your parent conferences. For most programs, these checkpoints will occur in the fall, about 6 weeks after the program begins; in mid-winter; in the spring; and in the summer if your program operates year-round. Some teachers like to use the *Observation Tracking Form* between checkpoints to record which children they have observed, when, and for what objectives.

 If you are using CreativeCurriculum.net, you enter and finalize Progress Checkpoints on a regular basis. Your observation notes will appear next to each objective to help you make decisions. Keeping Progress Checkpoints updated generates Individual Child Profiles and helps you plan.

Here is an excerpt from Willard's *Individual Child Profile*, showing his Objective 2 development over three checkpoint periods.

	social/emotional development

Goal 1: To learn about self and others

Objectives and Steps	CHECKPOINTS			
	F	W	Sp	Su
Objective 2: Regulates own behavior				
1. Begins developing own patterns for sleeping, eating, and other basic needs, with adult's help				
2. Uses others' facial expressions, gestures, or voices to guide own behavior	✓			
3. Begins to respond to verbal redirection		✓	✓	
4. Follows simple directions and sometimes tests limits				
5. Understands what behavior is expected, with increasing regularity				

Assessing Children With Disabilities

Assessing the progress of a child with a disability requires careful consideration of the objectives and steps. Consider how the child is progressing toward achieving the objective while using whatever modifications, adaptations, assistive devices, or assistive technologies are necessary. For example, a hearing-impaired child might use sign language rather than oral language to convey a message. If the child regularly combines two signs, you would record his skill level as Step 4, "Speaks in two-word phrases" of Objective 17, "Develops expressive language."

The same principle applies when evaluating a child with another kind of disability. For example, if a child's disability affects motor development, his step of Objective 8, "Demonstrates basic gross motor skills," would be assessed when he is using an assistive device such as a walker or wheelchair.

Thinking About Development After Thirty-Six Months

While the *Developmental Continuum for Infants, Toddlers & Twos* spans the ages from entry into your program to 36 months, some children might remain with you briefly beyond their third birthday. Sometimes even younger children show development beyond the steps of the *Developmental Continuum for Infants, Toddlers & Twos* for some objectives. Whatever the reason for their relative maturity, you will need a way to assess the children's continuing development and learning, and you will want to know what to expect in terms of next steps.

Each of the 21 objectives of *The Creative Curriculum Developmental Continuum for Infants, Toddlers & Twos* leads to one or more of the 50 objectives of *The Creative Curriculum Developmental Continuum for Ages 3–5*. Some of the objectives for infants, toddlers, and twos correlate directly with one objective for preschool-age children. For instance, Objective 12, "Shows a beginning understanding of cause and effect" corresponds with preschool Objective 25, "Explores cause and effect." However, most objectives of the continuum for infants, toddlers, and twos lead to several preschool objectives. The chart that follows shows how an objective for infants, toddlers, and twos provides the foundation for three preschool objectives.

Objective for Infants, Toddlers & Twos	Objectives for Preschoolers
17. Develops expressive language	39. Expresses self using words and expanded sentences 41. Answers questions 42. Asks questions

The chart on pages 30–32 shows the relationship between the two *Developmental Continuums*.

As children in your class reach age three, you may want to begin to use *The Creative Curriculum Developmental Continuum for Ages 3–5* as your instrument for ongoing assessment. If your program continues to use the *Developmental Continuum for Infants, Toddlers & Twos*, you may want to refer to the *Developmental Continuum for Ages 3–5* to see what next steps the children in your class are likely to take.

V. Planning for Each Child and the Group

The primary benefit of using the *The Creative Curriculum Developmental Continuum for Infants, Toddlers & Twos* Assessment System is that you collect a wealth of information that you can use to plan for each child and the group. The *Developmental Continuum* helps you appreciate what a child knows and can do, and it helps you consider the next steps in the child's development. This knowledge informs the many decisions you make as you implement *The Creative Curriculum*. Two weekly planning forms, the *Child Planning Form* and the *Group Planning Form*, are also available to help you prepare for each day and respond to children's changing interests and abilities.

Using the *Child Planning Form*

You can use the *Child Planning Form* on a weekly basis to record current information about each child in your primary care group. Look at your recent observation notes. Select key information to guide your plan for the week. Think about what the information means and record your plans on the form.

Here is an example of a *Child Planning Form* that was completed for a group of mobile infants.

◆ CREATIVE CURRICULUM®
FOR INFANTS, TODDLERS & TWOS

Child Planning Form

Teacher(s):	Grace
Group:	Infants
Week of:	February 2–6

Child: Abby (14 months)

Current information:
Abby has been filling purses with small toys and carrying them around. She's also starting to nap earlier in the morning.

Plans:
Add some small baskets to the room for filling and carrying. Adjust the schedule to accommodate new nap time.

Child: Max (16 months)

Current information:
Max played with two simple puzzles every day.

Plans:
Add two new knob puzzles and leave the old ones. Encourage him to discover and try the new ones.

Child: Devon (18 months)

Current information:
Devon enjoyed hearing The Itsy Bitsy Spider

Child: Shawntee (18 months)

Current information:
Shawntee needs to be by me when new

 If you are using CreativeCurriculum.net, you can include activities from the Activity Library in your *Child Planning Form.* You can also complete the form online and send it to your supervisor for feedback.

Using the *Group Planning Form*

The *Group Planning Form* helps you determine changes to the environment, the schedule, and routines. You record such things as what materials and special experiences to offer. Use the information you recorded about individual children on the *Child Planning Form*.

Here is an example of a *Group Planning Form* for the mobile infant group.

Group Planning Form

Teacher(s):	Grace
Group:	Infants
Week of:	February 2–6

Changes to the Environment:

Add a variety of small baskets (plastic and wicker)

Put out two new knob puzzles next to the familiar ones

Changes to Routines and Schedule:

Start going outside 15 minutes earlier in the morning, to accommodate new nap times

Family Involvement:

Max's dad is coming for the morning on Friday

Special Experiences I Plan to Offer This Week					
	Monday	**Tuesday**	**Wednesday**	**Thursday**	**Friday**
Indoor Experiences	Read *The Itsy Bitsy Spider* and use the puppet (all week)	Water play inside (small tubs with water and pouring cups)	Water play inside (small tubs with water and pouring cups)	Get ready for the picnic—help pack the picnic basket	Max's dad visits for the morning
Outdoor Experiences	Introduce the new climber	Use the new climber	Use the new climber	Morning picnic on the	Walk to the park

If you are using CreativeCurriculum.net, you can include activities from the Activity Library in your *Group Planning Form.* You can also complete the form online and send it to your supervisor for feedback.

Linking Curriculum and Assessment

The *Developmental Continuum* helps you acknowledge the amazing development and learning a child achieves during the first three years of life. As you use it to focus your observations of each child, think about and appreciate what he knows and can do. For example, when Leo insists on staying on Barbara's lap when a new person comes into the room to unclog the sink, he is using her as a secure base around new people (Objective 1, Step 3). When Jasmine raises her bottle as the level of milk drops, she is doing much more than getting a drink. She is starting to develop a beginning understanding of cause and effect (Objective 12, Step 2).

Using the *Developmental Continuum* will help you understand the significance of children's behaviors, which might otherwise puzzle you. You will also recognize and appreciate how much they are learning every day. The information will help you make decisions about each child and about all aspects of implementing *The Creative Curriculum for Infants, Toddlers & Twos*.

Here are some examples of how assessment information helps teachers make decisions related to curriculum. The box near each example refers you to the chapters in *The Creative Curriculum* where you can find more information and strategies. Although the children in your program may face developmental issues that are different from those described here—and you may therefore have to make different decisions—your approach to using information about each child will be the same.

Building relationships with children

How do I build a positive relationship with a child who cries a lot?

When I first met Julio, he fussed and cried a lot, no matter how hard I tried to calm him. It was hard for me to feel close to him. Then one day I picked him up when he was crying, and he relaxed and snuggled into my arms (Objective 1, "Trusts known, caring adults," Step 1, "Recognizes and reaches out to familiar adults"). *The* Developmental Continuum *helped me understand that Julio relaxed because he trusted me. I started to connect with him more, and I think he felt it. I spent more time with him when he wasn't crying. When he had a tough time, it was easier for him to let me comfort him.*

i For more information

Chapter 4, "Caring and Teaching," discusses strategies for building relationships with children.

Knowing and working with families

How do I address a family's concerns, help them recognize their child's strengths, and become partners in supporting their child's learning and development?

Leo's mother worried because he never sat still long enough to hear a story. We observed him together and saw that Leo likes to turn pages and point to pictures of people and familiar objects (Objective 19, "Enjoys books and being read to," Step 3, "Becomes increasingly engaged with the content of books that are read aloud.") Looking at the Developmental Continuum *helped her see that he was showing an interest in stories and books. Now we're making Leo a book with family photos.*

i For more information

Chapter 5, "Building Partnerships With Families," discusses strategies for working with families. Chapter 13, "Enjoying Stories and Books," talks about early literacy experiences.

Creating a welcoming environment

How do I show a family of a child with a disability that they are welcome and that their child's needs will be met?

Gena has cerebral palsy. Her parents were concerned about whether this was a good placement for her. On their first day, I showed them a wedge and how lying on it frees Gena's hands to explore and learn. A few days later, we observed Gena using hardwood blocks as cymbals (Objective 15, "Engages in Pretend Play," Step 4, "Substitutes one object for another in pretend play"). When her parents read the Developmental Continuum, *they understood that Gena was practicing fine motor skills, exploring materials, and beginning to substitute objects during her pretend play. With great relief, they said, "We are in the right place!"*

i For more information

Chapter 2, "Creating a Responsive Environment," offers strategies for creating a welcoming environment. Chapter 1, "Knowing Infants, Toddlers & Twos"; Chapter 2, "Creating a Responsive Environment"; and Chapter 4, "Caring and Teaching," include information about teaching children with disabilities.

Guiding behavior

How do I know what behavior to expect of children at different ages?

The Developmental Continuum *reminded me that young children need adult help as they learn to manage their behavior. Now I have more realistic expectations for Abby. When she started to hit a child in the sandbox the other day, I looked at her and shook my head, "No"* (Objective 2, "Regulates own behavior," Step 2, "Uses others' facial expressions, gestures, or voices to guide behavior"). *I explained that hitting hurts, and I sat with her, helping her fill a bucket with sand.*

i For more information

Chapter 1, "Knowing Infants, Toddlers & Twos," gives information about what young children are like. Chapter 4, "Caring and Teaching," discusses ways to guide children's behavior.

Shaping routines

How do I plan the day?

I used to be in a hurry to get to special activities. Now I allow plenty of time for daily routines: putting on coats to go outside, setting the table for lunch, using the potty, and washing hands. Now I see Valisha, Jonisha, and the other children beginning to accomplish more complex personal care skills (Objective 7, "Uses personal care skills," Step 5, "Does many complex personal care tasks successfully").

i For more information

Chapters 6–10 discuss daily routines, including hellos and good-byes, diapering and toileting, eating and mealtimes, sleeping and nap time, and getting dressed.

Planning opportunities for learning

How do I decide what materials, toys, and equipment to provide?

My observations indicate that Willard definitely handles objects to learn how they work (Objective 11, "Understands how objects can be used," Step 2, "Learns how objects work by handling them and watching others use them"). *Knowing this, I got the pop-up box out of the closet and put it on the floor for him to discover."*

i For more information

Chapters 11–18 discuss daily experiences, including playing with toys, imitating and pretending, enjoying stories and books, connecting with music and movement, creating with art, tasting and preparing food, exploring sand and water, and going outdoors. Chapter 2, "Creating a Responsive Environment," includes information about selecting and displaying materials.

Summarizing a Child's Progress

As described in Section IV, teachers usually complete an *Individual Child Profile* for each child at three or four checkpoints during the year: Fall, Winter, Spring, and, in year-round programs, Summer. This report is for your program's internal use. It is **not** designed to be shared with family members.

To communicate with families, use the *Family Conference Form*. This form allows you to summarize the information you collected during the checkpoint period by goal area. Select a few of the child's important accomplishments in each goal area that you want to highlight when you meet with families. Consider the objectives that are likely to be most (and least) important to particular families. For example, since you know that Abby's mother does not value independence in personal care skills (Objective 7), you choose another objective in that goal area, perhaps Objective 4, "Responds to others' feelings with growing empathy." Enter the information on the form. There is space to record information about favorite activities and special interests, situations that cause distress, special circumstances in the child's life, and special needs. There is also a place for family members' comments and space to record next steps at home and in the program.

 If you are using CreativeCurriculum.net, the *Family Conference Form* can be generated and customized online. By selecting the information that you want to share with families, you create a form that serves as a discussion guide for a family conference.

The form provides you with information to share with families. Remember to select some items from the child's portfolio, such as photographs or artwork, to share as these will also provide useful information to family members about children's development and learning. When you summarize a child's progress at three or four points during the year and meet with families to share information and plan together, you build a partnership that benefits each child for many years.

Meeting and Planning With Families

Although teachers and family members usually have a few minutes to talk at the beginning and end of the day, most teachers arrange formal conferences or home visits with the families of each child in their program at three or four times a year. These are times to sit together, uninterrupted, to talk as partners. During conferences, teachers and families share information, observations, and questions. They try to solve problems when necessary, and they always celebrate each child as an individual.

The first meeting is usually a time to begin to get to know one another, to share information you each have about the child, and to discuss goals for the year. If you have not already explained how you get to know and plan for each child, the first meeting is a good time to do so. During the next meeting or meetings, families and teachers typically discuss the child's progress, what is expected next in terms of development, and how to work together to support the child's learning. At the final conference, parents and teachers usually reflect on the child's overall progress and plan for the coming year.

Assuring families that you know their child and care about his well-being helps put them at ease and sets the stage for a helpful conference. One of the most effective ways to do this is to start by sharing an observation of something new, interesting, or delightful that their child has done or said. You may also want to ask family members questions such as "What kinds of activities do you and your child enjoy doing together now?" or "What catches your child's interest?" Your observations show that you want to know their child as an individual, and your questions will encourage families to share some of their observations.

Next, share the *Family Conference Form.* Highlight new discoveries their child has made and skills she has mastered. Offer specific examples from your observation notes or portfolio samples that help you talk about the child's exploration and discoveries. Instead of presenting a random list of the child's recent accomplishments, explain how the examples relate to curricular goals. This will be more meaningful for families. For example, some parents may be upset that their child sucks his thumb. Your explanation that this is how their child is learning to comfort himself and manage his own feelings will help them think about thumb sucking from a new perspective.

Relate the child's development and learning to the family's everyday life. A parent of a child who is beginning to move from place to place may be tired of chasing her around and may appreciate a little support. It also gives you a chance to remind the family to review their baby-proofing, now that their child is able to reach new places.

Throughout your discussion, encourage families to share their observations, questions, challenges, and joys. Make it clear that this is a time to exchange information. Explain that, by sharing what each of you know, you will both have the clearest possible picture of their child. Seek information that will help you complete together the sections of the form about the child's favorite activities and special interests, situations or experiences that cause distress, and special circumstances. This will allow you to work together to give the child the support he needs and deserves.

Talk together about next steps in their child's development and learning. Together with the family, complete the "Next Steps" section of the form. This will become your blueprint for working with each child during the next three months or so until the next checkpoint and conference. The form will be the starting point for your discussions during the next family conference.

VI. Promoting High-Quality Assessment

Programs should plan sufficient training and support to help teachers implement the Assessment System well. In addition to general training, we encourage training related to these two items:

- interrater reliability

- assessment in early intervention settings

Establishing Interrater Reliability in Your Program

To make sure that your information about the children will be useful, all teachers in your program must assess children in the same way. Interrater reliability means that, given the same information, such as a collection of objective observation notes and portfolio samples, all teachers come to the same conclusion about which developmental step most accurately describes a child's level of development and learning. We suggest that you follow this strategy to establish interrater reliability in your program:

- Review the goals, objectives, and steps of the *Developmental Continuum* with all teachers. Review the process of ongoing assessment that includes collecting, analyzing, and then evaluating facts. Make sure all teachers understand how to choose the step that best reflects the child's development (see page 17).

- Have pairs of teachers observe the same child and then compare their observation notes to make sure they present facts without interpreting them.

- Collect a set of observation notes and portfolio samples and review them as a team.

    Select an objective. Have each teacher review the information and decide the appropriate step for the child. If teachers have difficulty deciding which step to choose, have them compare their observations with the examples in the *Developmental Continuum*. Remind teachers that they do not have to observe the particular behaviors given as examples. They are looking for equivalent behaviors.

    Discuss responses. If teachers disagree, have each one explain why he or she selected the step. Resolve differences.

    Repeat with each objective.

    Repeat the entire process until you feel confident that you and your teaching team agree how to choose the steps that best describe the child's development.

Using the Assessment System in Early Intervention Settings

Early intervention programs can use both *The Creative Curriculum for Infants, Toddlers & Twos* and *The Creative Curriculum Developmental Continuum for Infants, Toddlers & Twos* to inform program planning, to monitor children's development and learning, and to report children's progress. The difference between their use in early intervention programs and other programs is that more people are involved in the assessment process when a child with disabilities is served by a team.

Federal law (Part C of the Individuals with Disabilities Education Improvement Act of 2004) requires that early intervention services be provided in a child's "natural environment," or in "home and community settings in which children without disabilities participate." In other words, early intervention services are to be provided where children typically spend most of their days, rather than in clinical settings that are not natural places for children to be. The natural environment for a young child is often the child's home. Other common natural environments include homes of friends or relatives, family child care homes, child care centers, and play groups. In some cases, the child receiving services is the only child in the natural environment; in other instances, other children are also present.

In early intervention programs, the various professionals who work with a child function as a team in partnership with the child's family. Team members observe the child over time and in various situations in these natural environments, communicating with each other about effective strategies and the child's progress. Using the *Developmental Continuum* and more specialized tools, early intervention service providers collaborate to observe and document children's learning in a systematic way. They also coordinate their analysis and evaluation of the information. As a team, they then plan and individualize the program and intervention services for the child.

During their visits with the child and family, team members work with the family in the context of regular activities. These activities are sometimes related to routines, such as eating, sleeping, diapering, or dressing and sometimes to experiences, such as taking a walk or playing with toys. While interacting with the child and family, service providers observe the child and document what they see and hear. They record their observations in a variety of ways, including photographs, video- and audiotapes, and written observation notes. Sometimes family members and service providers create a portfolio together and talk about what they learn about the child from the items.

Each early intervention team member plays a role in observing and documenting the child's behavior by using the *Developmental Continuum* during visits with the child and family. If a child's Individual Family Service Plan (IFSP) specifies that she is receiving education, speech-language, occupational, and physical therapies, and social work services, each team member takes responsibility for observing and documenting the child's development in a specific developmental area. The speech-language pathologist focuses on language development, the occupational and physical therapists focus on physical development, and the educator focuses on cognitive development and, along with the social worker, also considers the child's social/emotional development. However, their observation notes often describe the child's behavior and skills related to other developmental areas, so sharing information is essential to understanding and supporting the child.

In *The Creative Curriculum for Infants, Toddlers & Twos*, planning and assessment are linked. You use the information you gain through the process of ongoing assessment to support your implementation of the curriculum in a way that best meets the strengths and needs of children and families. At the same time, you are building positive relationships with children and families and strengthening your skills as a teacher. With your support, the children in your care will thrive.

THE CREATIVE CURRICULUM®

FOR INFANTS, TODDLERS & TWOS

Goals and Objectives
At a Glance

SOCIAL/EMOTIONAL DEVELOPMENT	PHYSICAL DEVELOPMENT	COGNITIVE DEVELOPMENT	LANGUAGE DEVELOPMENT
To learn about self and others	**To learn about moving**	**To learn about the world**	**To learn about communicating**
1. Trusts known, caring adults	8. Demonstrates basic gross motor skills	10. Sustains attention	16. Develops receptive language
2. Regulates own behavior	9. Demonstrates basic fine motor skills	11. Understands how objects can be used	17. Develops expressive language
3. Manages own feelings		12. Shows a beginning understanding of cause and effect	18. Participates in conversations
4. Responds to others' feelings with growing empathy		13. Shows a beginning understanding that things can be grouped	19. Enjoys books and being read to
5. Plays with other children		14. Uses problem-solving strategies	20. Shows an awareness of pictures and print
6. Learns to be a member of a group		15. Engages in pretend play	21. Experiments with drawing and writing
7. Uses personal care skills			

Relationship Between the Objectives of *The Creative Curriculum Developmental Continuum for Infants, Toddlers & Twos* and *The Creative Curriculum Developmental Continuum for Ages 3–5*

Objectives for Infants, Toddlers & Twos	Objectives for Preschoolers
1. Trusts known, caring adults	1. Shows ability to adjust to new situations 2. Demonstrates appropriate trust in adults
2. Regulates own behavior	4. Stands up for rights 6. Takes responsibility for own well-being 13. Uses thinking skills to resolve conflicts
3. Manages own feelings	3. Recognizes own feelings and manages them appropriately
4. Responds to others' feelings with growing empathy	11. Recognizes the feelings of others and responds appropriately
5. Plays with other children	10. Plays well with other children 12. Shares and respects the rights of others
6. Learns to be a member of a group	7. Respects and cares for classroom environment and materials 8. Follows classroom routines 9. Follows classroom rules 10. Plays well with other children 12. Shares and respects the rights of others 13. Uses thinking skills to resolve conflicts
7. Uses personal care skills	5. Demonstrates self-direction and independence 6. Takes responsibility for own well-being

Objectives for Infants, Toddlers & Twos	Objectives for Preschoolers
8. Demonstrates basic gross motor skills	14. Demonstrates basic locomotor skills
	15. Shows balance while moving
	16. Climbs up and down
	17. Pedals and steers a tricycle (or other wheeled vehicle)
	18. Demonstrates throwing, kicking, and catching skills
9. Demonstrates basic fine motor skills	19. Controls small muscles in hands
	20. Coordinates eye-hand movement
	21. Uses tools for writing and drawing
10. Sustains attention	22. Observes objects and events with curiosity
	23. Approaches problems flexibly
	24. Shows persistence in approaching tasks
11. Understands how objects can be used	22. Observes objects and events with curiosity
12. Shows a beginning understanding of cause and effect	25. Explores cause and effect
13. Shows a beginning understanding that things can be grouped	22. Observes objects and events with curiosity
	27. Classifies objects
	28. Compares/measures
	29. Arranges objects in a series
	30. Recognizes patterns and can repeat them
	31. Shows awareness of time concepts and sequence
	32. Shows awareness of position in space
	33. Uses one-to-one correspondence
	34. Uses numbers and counting
14. Uses problem-solving strategies	23. Approaches problems flexibly
	24. Shows persistence in approaching tasks
	25. Explores cause and effect
	26. Applies knowledge or experience to a new context

Objectives for Infants, Toddlers & Twos	Objectives for Preschoolers
15. Engages in pretend play	35. Takes on pretend roles and situations
	36. Makes believe with objects
	37. Makes and interprets representations
16. Develops receptive language	38. Hears and discriminates the sounds of language
	40. Understands and follows oral directions
	41. Answers questions
	48. Comprehends and interprets meaning from books and other texts
17. Develops expressive language	39. Expresses self using words and expanded sentences
	41. Answers questions
	42. Asks questions
18. Participates in conversations	43. Actively participates in conversations
19. Enjoys books and being read to	44. Enjoys and values reading
20. Shows an awareness of pictures and print	45. Demonstrates understanding of print concepts
	46. Demonstrates knowledge of the alphabet
	47. Uses emerging reading skills to make meaning from print
21. Experiments with drawing and writing	21. Uses tools for writing and drawing
	37. Makes and interprets representations
	49. Understands the purpose of writing
	50. Writes letters and words